YOU CHOOSE
BOOKS™

WORLD WAR II
PILOTS

An Interactive History Adventure

by Michael Burgan

Consultant:
Dennis Showalter, PhD
Professor of History
Colorado College

CAPSTONE PRESS
a capstone imprint

You Choose Books are published by Capstone Press,
1710 Roe Crest Drive, North Mankato, Minnesota 56003
www.capstonepub.com

Library of Congress Cataloging-in-Publication Data
Burgan, Michael.
    World War II pilots : an interactive history adventure / by Michael Burgan.
        p. cm. — (You choose books: World War II)
    Summary: "Describes the role pilots played during World War II. Readers' choices
reveal various historical details"—Provided by publisher.
    Includes bibliographical references and index.
    ISBN 978-1-4296-9899-3 (library binding)
    ISBN 978-1-62065-718-8 (paperback)
    ISBN 978-1-4765-7685-5 (paperback)
    ISBN 978-1-4765-1813-8 (ebook PDF)
1. World War, 1939-1945—Aerial operations—Juvenile literature. I. Title.
D785.B87 2013
940.54'4—dc23   2012028703

Editorial Credits
Kristen Mohn, editor; Bobbie Nuytten, designer; Wanda Winch, media researcher;
Jennifer Walker, production specialist

Photo Credits
akg-images: ullstein bild, 29; Alamy: Danita Delimont, 90, DIZ Muenchen GmbH, Suddeutsche
Zeitung Photo, 23, GL Archive, 54, Lordprice Collection, 16; AP Images: U.S. Army/Wever,
cover; Corbis, 9, Hulton-Deutsch Collection, 40, 103, Sygma/John Van Hasselt, 70; Courtesy of
Ingrid Dockter, WW II dog tags used as design element; Getty Images Inc: Time Life Images/
William Vandivert, 39; Library of Congress: Prints and Photographs Division, 65, 72, 98;
MaritimeQuest: Michael W. Pocock/Frank A. Stockwell, R.N. Collection, 100; National Archives
and Records Administration, 12, 45, 57, 63; Rex USA: Associated Newspapers, 33; Shutterstock:
Andrey Kuzmin, steel plate background, Darren Brode, 49, Nella, metal texture background; U.S.
Air Force photo, 83, Toni Frissell, 77; USAFA McDermott Library SMS 329, 89
Printed in China.
042013   007322

TABLE OF CONTENTS

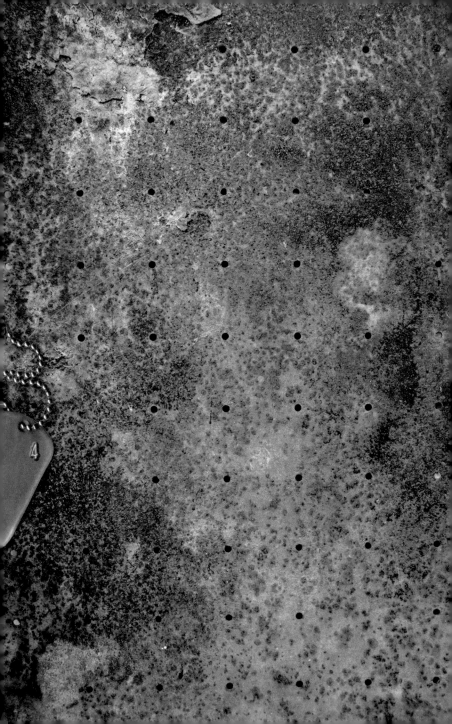

ABOUT YOUR ADVENTURE

YOU are living through World War II. It's the early 1940s and airplanes, including bombers and fighters, are playing a major role in battle. You want to join the fight.

In this book you'll explore how the choices people made meant the difference between life and death. The events you'll experience happened to real people.

Chapter One sets the scene. Then you choose which path to read. Follow the directions at the bottom of each page. The choices you make will change your outcome. After you finish your path, go back and read the others for new perspectives and more adventures.

YOU CHOOSE the path
you take through history.

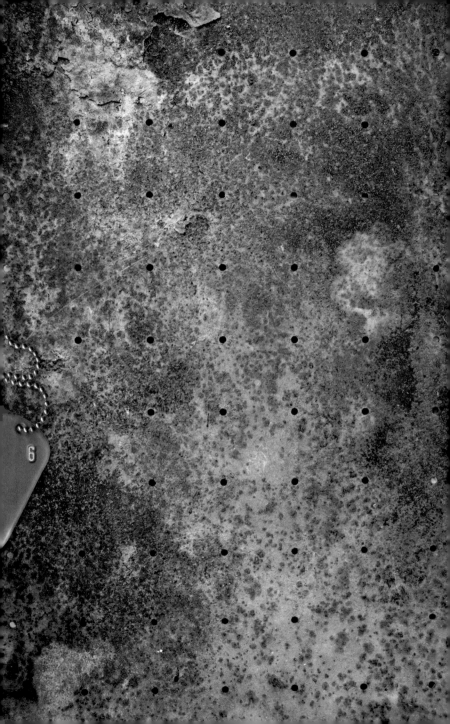

WARFARE IN THE SKIES

World War II started in 1939 and involves dozens of countries. The war's roots are deep, going back to the end of World War I in 1918.

In World War I the winning countries called themselves the Allies. They blamed Germany for starting the war and wanted to punish it afterward. Germany had to give up some of its land and its military. The Allies, particularly France and Great Britain, also demanded that Germany pay for the damage it caused during the war.

7

Through the 1920s Germany became angry over this treatment. In 1933 a new leader came to power in Germany—Adolf Hitler. He promised to make Germany a strong, powerful nation again. He also wanted to punish people he thought had weakened Germany. This included the country's Jewish citizens. He and his Nazi Party took away Jews' legal rights and sent them to prison camps.

Through the 1930s Germany secretly strengthened its military—including building a huge new air force. Then, starting in 1936, Hitler sent troops into parts of Europe where Germans lived, claiming the land for his country. Germany's invasion of Poland in September 1939 marked the beginning of World War II.

German soldiers marched in a victory parade after the invasion of Poland.

Italy, which became a partner of Germany, also wanted to spread its control. Italian leader Benito Mussolini sent troops into part of North Africa. In Asia, Japan was making a similar grab for new land. The Japanese, like the Germans and Italians, thought they had the right to rule other countries.

Turn the page.

By 1939 military planners around the world saw airplanes as a key weapon. Planes were used to bring troops into battle as well as attack enemy forces. And the development of aircraft carriers—ships that carry aircraft—meant planes could carry out attacks far in the ocean.

On December 7, 1941, Japanese warplanes bombed the U.S. naval base at Pearl Harbor, Hawaii. The planes killed more than 2,000 Americans. The United States quickly declared war on Japan. Japan's partners, Italy and Germany, then declared war on the United States.

The countries of Germany, Italy, and Japan are known as the Axis powers. The Allies in this war are countries that oppose the Axis, including the United States, France, Poland, Great Britain, and many others as the war progresses.

As the war builds, you feel called to duty. You want to help defend your country—and you want to do it in the skies. You decide to become a pilot.

• *To be a British pilot in the Royal Air Force, turn to page 13.*

• *To be an American pilot fighting in the Pacific Ocean, turn to page 41.*

• *To be a member of the Tuskegee Airmen, turn to page 73.*

Firefighters put out flames from German bombs during the Battle of Britain.

CHAPTER 2

THE BATTLE OF BRITAIN

It's September 1939 and your town in Great Britain is in an uproar. German troops invaded Poland, and British leaders have promised to help the Poles. Your country declares war on Germany.

Your parents have heard the news about the war. Your father tells you, "With the war coming, you have to sign up for National Service. That means you could be called up for the military."

"I know," you say. "But I don't want to wait. I want to volunteer for the Royal Air Force."

"A pilot!" your mother wails. "Why do you want to risk your life in the RAF?"

"You know I've always wanted to fly," you reply.

13

Turn the page.

Your mother fights back tears and looks at your father. "He could ask for a deferment, since we need him here on the farm," your father says. Your mother nods and looks at you.

You know your parents count on you. But so does your country. Germany might even invade Britain some day, just like it did Poland. You want to defend your homeland.

• To seek a deferment, go to page 15.

• To volunteer for the RAF, turn to page 20.

Your deferment is approved, but you still often think about flying. Not much fighting takes place in Europe for the rest of the year. Then in the spring of 1940, Hitler's armies begin to move again. On the radio you hear about the invasion of Norway and Denmark. Next, Belgium and the Netherlands are captured. And by June the Germans have taken France as well. You wonder if Britain will be next.

An attack finally comes in August. German planes attack the RAF aerodrome at Manston Air Base. Germany's continued air assault is soon known as the Battle of Britain. Soon the Germans have changed their targets. Instead of bombing military bases like Manston, they've switched to Britain's largest cities, including London.

Turn the page.

You decide you have to act. You volunteer for the RAF and begin training. Just as you had hoped, you're learning to fly a fighter plane. And what a plane it is—the Spitfire, the newest and fastest British fighter. In it, you can soar at more than 350 miles per hour. You pass all your tests, are assigned to your squadron, and begin flying in missions.

The Spitfire's great speed allowed it to fly deep into enemy territory and escape quickly.

After a recent mission, you told the mechanic, Burt, that your engine wasn't working right. You've got another mission today, but Burt hasn't had time to fix it yet. You probably shouldn't fly it. "Maybe you can take Henderson's plane," Burt says. "He's too sick to fly."

You know exactly how your plane flies. You'll feel more comfortable in it. But it could be dangerous to fly before it is repaired.

• To take Henderson's plane, turn to page 18.

• To fly your own plane, turn to page 26.

17

You climb into Henderson's plane, take off down the runway, and head for the German planes approaching the coast. A voice comes in over your radio. "Bandits at 5,000 feet," the controller says, referring to enemy planes. "Looks like Me 109s."

"I see them," you say. You line up the closest Messerschmitt 109 in your gun sight and press the gun button. Nothing happens! You press again and again, but still no bullets. In the confusion of switching to Henderson's plane, the armorer forgot to load the machine guns!

You turn again as the Me 109 shoots at you. Some of the bullets rip into your plane. They don't cause serious damage, though, and you fly on. But you can't do much to stop the Me 109s if you don't have any bullets.

You're just about to head back to base when you see one of the enemy planes closing in on another Spitfire. You know the pilot—Archie Nelson. You want to help him, but you're not sure what you can do without bullets.

• To try to help Archie, turn to page 29.

• To go back to base, turn to page 32.

You look at your parents. "I'm sorry, Mum, Dad," you say. "I'm going to join the RAF."

You start weeks of training in the classroom. Each day starts before 6 a.m. You study math and learn how to navigate. Outside, you do fast marches across the camp or go on long runs. You face extra drills outside if you disobey any rules.

Through all this early training, you don't even get inside a plane. And you still have more weeks ahead in the classroom. You begin to wonder if you've made the right decision. Maybe you should have asked for that deferment.

• To stay in the RAF, go to page 21.

• To leave the RAF, turn to page 34.

You decide to work harder. After classroom training, you go to a new base where you finally start to fly. You climb into a Tiger Moth, a biplane designed to teach new pilots. An instructor flies with you in a second cockpit. After just 15 flight hours with him, he lets you fly solo.

After several months more training, you earn your wings—you're an RAF pilot. You're given a choice of which fighter to fly: a Spitfire or a Hurricane.

"The Spitfire is a beauty," your friend Tom says. "And fast."

"But the Hurricane is solid," you say. "If a German fighter blasts at you, the Hurricane can take a lot of bullets and keep on flying."

• To fly a Spitfire, turn to page 22.

• To fly a Hurricane, turn to page 37.

"I'll take speed over strength," you say. "After all, if the German planes can't catch you, they can't hurt you. I'll take the Spitfire."

By now it's the summer of 1940. While you're training, German troops are moving across western Europe. In June they seize France. Everyone is sure Great Britain will be Hitler's next target.

By August the Germans are sending hundreds of bombers to attack Britain. It's your mission to stop them. Joining you are fellow pilots from across the British Empire—New Zealand, Canada, Australia. Others are from countries the Nazis have defeated, such as Czechoslovakia and Poland. Your commander assigns you as Red Two, one of three planes in your section.

Thanks to the new invention of radar, you know that German planes are heading for major cities along the coast. You head in that direction and discover that the planes are German bombers called Heinkel 111s. These He 111 bombers lack much firepower. But you know they don't fly alone. Somewhere close by are German fighters, most likely Messerschmitt 109s.

An He 111 bombardier used a bombsight and maps to find targets.

Turn the page.

You want to attack the Me 109 fighters first, then come back for the bombers before they reach the coast. "Red Two, Red Two," you hear over your radio. "Bandits down below."

Now you see a group of six Me 109s. You and the other two planes swoop down to attack. In a moment your Spitfire is shaking from the force of all your machine guns firing at once.

Your bullets score a direct hit. Black smoke streams from one of the German planes. You turn to attack another Me 109. This time the enemy pilot fires first.

One explosive bullet rips into your cockpit, and tiny pieces of metal strike your arm. You grit your teeth but keep going. With a roll of your plane, you come up behind the Me 109. Another blast of your guns sends this one down too.

The other planes in your squadron have taken care of the rest of the fighters. Now you close in on an He 111. You take aim at one of its two engines. After a short blast of your guns, the bomber's engine begins to smoke. But maybe you should fire again, to make sure you've gotten it.

• To let the He 111 land, turn to page 35.

• To attack again, turn to page 36.

No matter the danger, you'll feel better being in your own plane. "Does anyone else know about the engine?" you ask Burt. He shakes his head no. "Good. Don't tell them."

As you slide the hood shut, Burt calls out, "If your engine cuts out, you might not get it back."

You wave, then head off down the runway. The Blitz, as this part of the Battle of Britain is called, has led to thousands of deaths. But you and the other British pilots have an advantage—radar. This new invention lets radio stations on the ground detect German planes when they take off. You and the other fighters know where the enemy is heading.

Down below you see a group of German fighter planes—Me 109s. The German fighter is just as fast as your Spitfire, and it carries better guns. It can also climb and dive faster than the Spitfire, but the Spitfire can turn quicker. You've had dogfights before with Me 109s and always survived. You begin to move down to attack one of the enemy planes.

You fly behind an Me 109 and begin to fire your machine guns. A direct hit! But as you watch that plane spiral down to the ground, two more Me 109s come toward you. You begin to dive, but your engine cuts out. The dive has cut off the flow of gas to your engine—one problem with the Spitfire. Normally the gas flows again, but not this time.

Turn the page.

You remember what Burt said, as the enemy bullets hit your plane. Your cockpit fills with smoke. Coughing and struggling to breathe, you release the hatch and jump into the sky. You pull the cord on your parachute and begin to catch your breath. But just when you think you're out of danger, you're stabbed with a blinding pain. Bullets from an Me 109 rip into you as you fall. You're dead before you hit the ground.

28

THE END

To follow another path, turn to page 11.
To read the conclusion, turn to page 101.

The Messerschmitt 109 was the most important fighter in the *Luftwaffe*, Germany's air force.

You radio Archie and tell him to look out for the approaching Me 109. You and the German plane are heading right for one another, nose to nose. The only difference is that his guns are working. He fires. More bullets rip into your Spitfire, but somehow they miss your engine and other important parts.

Turn the page.

At that last instant, you put the nose down and try to pass underneath the Me 109. But it's too late and you're too close. With the deafening crash of metal on metal, you collide with the Me 109.

The cockpit immediately fills with smoke. Flames begin to leap from the engine. You try to open the hood, but the metal holding it in place is too damaged. There's no way to parachute out.

You have only one hope: crash-land the Spitfire. The plane is already diving downward. You pull up on the stick and try to regain control. Through the smoke, you can tell you are flying over land. You aim for a flat area and hope for the best.

Your speed is down to about 100 miles per hour when you hit. You bounce around in the cockpit as the plane plows through wooden fence posts. At last the plane comes to a rest.

The hood, though, still won't open. Flames are pouring out of the engine. You reach for the crowbar all the Spitfires have and strike the glass with it. You squeeze out of the cockpit, cutting your arms and legs. As you stagger away, you look back to see the whole plane go up in flames.

You look up and see more Me 109s closing in on Archie. You watch with horror as his plane explodes from German gunfire. You're alive, but your friend is dead. You'll always regret that you couldn't save him.

THE END

To follow another path, turn to page 11.
To read the conclusion, turn to page 101.

It's too dangerous to help Archie. As you head back to base, you see a German Me 110 approach—another fighter. Its cannons are powerful, but your plane can turn sharper and faster in a dogfight.

The Me 110 comes barreling toward you, its cannons blazing. You dive and roll and use all your skills to dodge the shots. But some still find their mark, ripping into your plane and damaging your rudder.

You dive down, hoping the other pilot will think you're going to crash. The Me 110 flies off. Just in time, you pull back on the stick to come out of your dive and head back to base. As soon as you land, you plan to have a talk with the armorer who forgot to load the guns.

The next day you learn that Archie didn't make it. The news hits you like a punch to the stomach. You are sad to know he's gone. But you're also proud of him—you know he went down fighting.

RAF pilot gear included parachutes, harnesses, and warm sheepskin flying jackets.

THE END

To follow another path, turn to page 11.
To read the conclusion, turn to page 101.

The next day you talk to your sergeant. You tell him you're not sure you still want to be a pilot.

"Plenty of trainees wash out and don't get their wings," he says. "But you said you wanted to be part of the RAF. We'll see about getting you another job. We need navigators and radio operators."

The sergeant is right. You asked to join. You realize you'll just have to try your best through the rest of the training and do what you can to help fight the Germans.

THE END

To follow another path, turn to page 11.
To read the conclusion, turn to page 101.

You pull alongside the He 111 and try to flag the pilot. More smoke is pouring out, and you know he'll never reach his target. You point to the ground and mouth the words, "Go down! Land!" The German pilot sees you and nods. He understands that you will let him land rather than shoot him down.

You watch as he lands and a police car races up. The German crew will be taken as prisoners of war. As you fly over the men, the bomber pilot waves. You are enemies, but you still respect one another. You head back to base, knowing you will have more missions to fly before the day is done.

THE END

To follow another path, turn to page 11.
To read the conclusion, turn to page 101.

You circle up and over the He 111 to come at it from behind. You fire another round of bullets. These hit the other engine, and soon the German bomber is crashing below you.

"Got him!" you yell. But your celebration doesn't last long. Just as you're turning to look for another bomber, an Me 109 comes at you, blasting. You're hit! You have only seconds to prepare for your death as your Spitfire plummets to the ground in flames. You die on impact, just yards from the German bomber you shot down.

36

THE END

To follow another path, turn to page 11.
To read the conclusion, turn to page 101.

"I like the idea of surviving enemy fire," you say. You go with the Hurricane.

One rainy day in August, you head out on a mission. You spy German bombers called Dornier 17s. With the Do 17s is a group of fighters. Your plane is in the first group of Hurricanes closing in for the attack.

Before you can fire your guns, tracers from the Me 109s streak past you. Your plane's been hit! You have only a few seconds to act before flames fill the cockpit.

Turn the page.

Your pants catch fire as you release the hood of the plane to parachute out. Immediately you feel the searing heat reach your skin. In a panic, you leap. The rushing air puts out the flames on your clothing. You sigh in relief as your parachute brings you safely to the ground.

When you land, local men with shotguns are waiting for you. "Don't shoot!" you scream. "I'm British!" You pull your ID card out of your charred pants. As you are driven to the base, you realize how badly your legs are burned. But the wounds are worth it, if you can help defeat the Nazis.

38

THE END

To follow another path, turn to page 11.
To read the conclusion, turn to page 101.

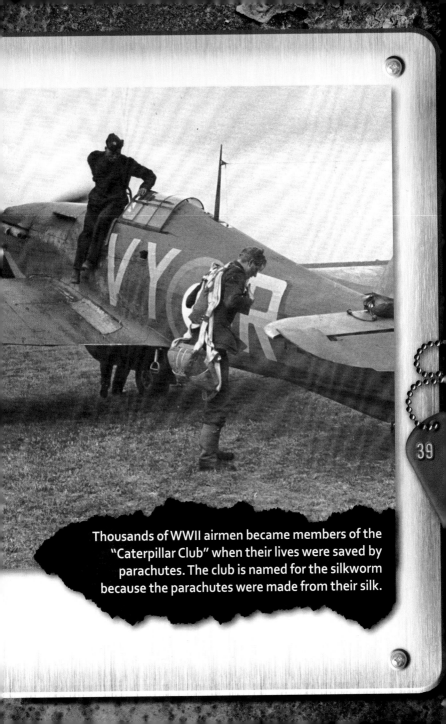

Thousands of WWII airmen became members of the "Caterpillar Club" when their lives were saved by parachutes. The club is named for the silkworm because the parachutes were made from their silk.

An American bomber crew prepared for a mission.

CHAPTER 3

FLYING IN THE PACIFIC

You were still in high school when the Japanese bombed Pearl Harbor in 1941. You wanted to fight, but you were too young. Now it's 1944. You're done with school and ready to do your part. You want to become a pilot. You and your friend Jimmy plan to enlist together.

"Should we join the Navy or the Army?" Jimmy asks.

"Those Navy fighter pilots have the Hellcat," you say. "I'd love to fly one of those. It can do almost 400 miles per hour!" You know that Navy pilots flying Hellcats have been scoring many kills against the Zero, the top Japanese fighter.

41

"But the Army Air Force has some great planes too," Jimmy says. "The P-51 Mustang is even faster than the Hellcat. You could fly along to protect those big bombers that are really doing damage to Germany. Or maybe fly a bomber yourself, and attack some Japanese ships."

• To join the Navy, go to page 43.

• To join the Army Air Force, turn to page 50.

"I've always wanted to go to sea," you say. "And I've always wanted to fly. I think being a Navy pilot is the best bet for me."

Your training starts at a naval air station. From there the Navy sends you to a training school run by civilians to see if you can handle a small aircraft. After some lessons you fly a Piper Cub, a two-seat trainer. The Cub is tiny and slow compared to the Hellcats you hope to fly. But in it you convince the Navy you have the skills needed to be a pilot.

You move on to the University of Iowa, where the Navy has a preflight training school. Over several months, you learn how to operate a radio and navigate a plane.

Turn the page.

Your next stop is a flight training school in Florida. After months of hard work, you earn your wings—you are a Navy pilot. Now you will complete your training on the plane you'll fly in combat. All along you've been thinking about flying the Hellcat fighter. But now you realize how important torpedo bombers are too.

One of the bombers Navy pilots fly in the Pacific is the Avenger. The Avenger can take out enemy ships, and its machine guns are powerful enough to shoot down Japanese planes.

44

• To fly the Avenger torpedo bomber, go to page 45.

• To fly the Hellcat fighter, turn to page 48.

The USS *San Jacinto* carried 45 aircraft and more than 1,500 men.

45

You pick the Avenger. It has a radioman and a gunner, and you like the idea of flying with a crew.

Early in 1945 you are assigned to the aircraft carrier *San Jacinto*. Each day you practice taking off and landing on a moving ship.

Turn the page.

In February you're assigned your first combat flight. Your ship is part of a major assault on the Japanese island of Iwo Jima. You take off with your usual crew. Buddy is the radioman, and Ted is the gunner. You are separated from your crew by a metal plate, so you communicate by radio.

You carry bombs as you head for the island. As you approach, black smoke from Japanese anti-aircraft guns fills the air. Even with the smoke, you manage to find your target and drop your 500-pound bombs.

"I think we got them!" you say, squinting to see through the smoke below. But as you circle the Avenger to head back to the ship, anti-aircraft fire rips into the plane. Your cockpit fills with smoke. Gasping for air, you radio to the crew, "We've been hit! Get ready to jump!"

Neither Buddy nor Ted radios back. What if they've been injured? Should you leave the plane without checking?

• To parachute out, turn to page 58.

• To check on your crew, turn to page 59.

After training you're assigned to a new aircraft carrier, the USS *Randolph*. In January 1945 it sails out of San Francisco for Ulithi, an island thousands of miles away in the Pacific.

As you sail you practice an aerial move called the Thach Weave. It helps American pilots avoid getting shot down by the best Japanese fighter plane, the Zero.

A pilot named Frank works with you on the Thach Weave. He's an "ace," which means that he's shot down at least five enemy planes. "We fly side by side," Frank explains, "but spaced apart. If a Zero comes up on our tail, we start to crisscross each other. The Zero will pick one of us to follow—and the other one of us will have a clear shot at him."

When the *Randolph* reaches Ulithi, you receive your orders. You and other fighter pilots will fly with bombers sent to attack Japan.

The Mitsubishi A6M Zero, a long-range fighter used by the Japanese, had a flying range of more than 1,200 miles.

49

Turn to page 56.

Jimmy is right—the Army has great planes too. You go with him to an Army recruiting office. After taking tests and a physical exam, you get the good word—you've both made it. But the road to actually flying is a long one. And you receive some bad news. At 6 feet, you're too tall for the 5-foot 8-inch height limit to fly the Mustang fighter. Maybe being a bomber pilot won't be so bad.

You and Jimmy take a train to the Army Air Force base in Santa Ana, California. At the base you go through more training and testing. The tests are hard, but both of you make it.

Then you head to another California base for flight training. The training is intense. About 25 percent of the cadets drop out of the program.

After months of hard work, you and Jimmy earn your wings. Now you'll go for your final training on the planes you'll fly in combat. You'll be flying one of the bombers, either a B-24 or B-25.

The B-24 has four engines, so it can take a lot of engine damage and keep flying. But that plane is strictly a high-altitude bomber, and it requires an oxygen mask. The B-25 can go on various missions, including hunting enemy submarines and scouting out enemy activity.

• To fly a B-24, turn to page 52.

• To fly a B-25, turn to page 64.

You finish your final training on a B-24. Then your squadron heads to a base in India, which is a British colony. From there your squadron begins to carry out bombing missions. You'll be attacking Japanese bases in Burma, a country between India and China.

Unlike most bombers, you fly without fighter planes to protect you. The route is too far for the fighters. They can't carry enough fuel. But your B-24 has 10 machine guns positioned around the plane. Along with your gunners, your crew includes a co-pilot, a navigator, a radio operator, and a bombardier.

One night your plane takes off, heading for railways the Japanese use to move supplies. You reach the target and drop your bombs. But on the way back, several Japanese fighters approach.

You hear tracers streak past the plane. These bullets have chemicals inside that create a trail of smoke. The whistling sound is followed by the loud rat-a-tat of your guns firing back. Then you hear a cry—Roy, a gunner, has been hit by enemy bullets.

"We've got a bandit right on our tail," your co-pilot, Bill, says.

Your B-24 is too slow to outrun the Zero. You think about how to shake him—if you can.

"Look at those mountains ahead," Joe, the navigator, calls. "I can guide you down low enough so we might be able to get that Zero to crash into them."

"But if we go too low, we could crash too," Bill says.

• To fly toward the mountain, turn to page 54.

• To turn away from the mountain, turn to page 67.

You begin to lower the B-24, to get closer to the approaching mountain. The Zero has to stay about 400 feet beneath you to get into the best position to attack. You're hoping that in the darkness he can't see the mountain ahead of you. You follow the navigator's directions as he guides you close to the mountainside. Closer, closer—and you zoom over the rocky peak. A second later you glance back and see a huge ball of fire fill the night sky.

The Allies used thousands of B-24 Liberators during WWII against enemy targets.

"It worked!" Bill says. Over the radio you hear the crew cheering. You head back to base while the bombardier takes care of Roy. He's going to be all right, and you and your crew have survived another mission.

The next day a general approaches you. He heard about your bravery the night before. "We need good pilots like you in other parts of Asia," he says. "We have a secret mission you might want to consider. Or, if you're open for learning something new, you can fly a B-25 in the Philippines."

55

• To go to the Philippines, turn to page 64.

• To accept the secret mission, turn to page 69.

You climb into your cockpit. Frank walks by and leans in before getting into his plane. "You're my wingman," he says. You nod and give him the thumbs up.

You and your squadron head for Tokyo. As you near the target, you see Zeroes approaching you. They want to lure the Hellcats away from the bombers, so other Zeroes can attack the bombers. But everyone in your squadron follows orders and stays with the Avengers. Closer to the target, though, dozens more Zeroes are waiting.

You fly toward the Zeroes and right away are surrounded. You twist and turn to avoid one Zero and find yourself on the tail of another. With a burst from your machine guns, one Zero goes down.

To the left you see a Zero closing in on Frank's plane. But in the other direction, a pack of Zeroes is heading for several Avengers. No other fighters are around to protect the bombers. Do you help your friend, or help the bombers carry out their mission?

Crewmen used catapults to launch aircraft, including Hellcats, into flight.

• To help Frank, turn to page 60.

• To help the Avengers, turn to page 61.

You hate to leave your crew, but your instincts tell you to save yourself. You get your parachute ready and open the cockpit. Now you see the wings are on fire. "I hope Buddy and Ted get out OK," you think, as you leap from the burning plane. After a few seconds, you pull the cord that opens the parachute. There's no sign of your crew.

You make a hard landing into the Pacific Ocean. Your life vest keeps you on the surface as you fumble to open your raft. Now, all you can do is hope a U.S. ship rescues you soon. As you drift in the sea, you think about Buddy and Ted, knowing they must have been killed. You'll always wonder if you could have saved them.

58

THE END

To follow another path, turn to page 11.
To read the conclusion, turn to page 101.

You radio Ted and Buddy again. This time you hear a faint sound—Buddy's voice. "I've been hit," he says. "Ted too. We can't jump, but you go."

"Not a chance, Buddy," you say. "Prepare for a water landing." You bring the Avenger down low toward the ocean, cutting the speed. With a thud the plane lands in the water. "Can you get out?" you radio to Buddy.

"I think so, but we might need some help."

But then you see a Japanese ship approaching. Sailors on deck are pointing guns at you. You've survived the crash, but now all three of you are about to become prisoners of war.

THE END

To follow another path, turn to page 11.
To read the conclusion, turn to page 101.

You open up the throttle all the way and speed toward the Zero that's attacking Frank. He radios to you, "Get in position so we can weave!"

As the Zero tries to get behind Frank, you start the Thach Weave. After a few crosses, you have the Zero right in front of you. You fire ahead of the plane, to the spot where you expect it to be in a split second. Your bullets hit their target. The Zero bursts into flames.

You're close enough now to see Frank in his cockpit. "Pretty soon you'll be an ace like me," he radios.

The bombers have hit their targets. It's time to head back to the *Randolph*. Maybe you'll become an ace on your next mission.

THE END

To follow another path, turn to page 11.
To read the conclusion, turn to page 101.

60

You're sure that Frank will be OK. The Avengers need you more. You see them firing their guns, trying to shoot down the much faster and sharper-turning Zeroes attacking them.

You close in on the nearest Zero, so your machine guns will be in range. Your bullets blast into the engine, sending the plane down. Now Frank and several other Hellcats have joined you in defending the Avengers. Together you shoot down two more enemy planes. The rest fly off before you can get them. You stick with the Avengers as they bomb their targets, and then you all return to the *Randolph*.

61

Turn the page.

For several weeks you don't fly any missions. The *Randolph* anchors at Ulithi. On the night of March 11, the pilots and sailors watch a movie called *A Song to Remember* on the hangar deck. Just as the movie is ending, you hear the noise of a single plane approaching the ship. Through the darkness you can't tell what it is, but you have a bad feeling.

It's a kamikaze! And it's coming straight for the ship with the aim to kill as many as possible.

The Japanese know they are losing the war in the Pacific. They've begun using kamikazes to attack U.S. ships. These bomb-loaded planes fly into their targets, exploding on impact. The Japanese pilots know they will die as they try to carry out their mission.

The USS *Randolph* docked alongside a repair ship after it was damaged by a kamikaze.

Within seconds it hits. A fiery explosion shakes the ship, and a piece of metal tears into your leg. You scream as you collapse on the deck. Through the smoke you see Frank crumpled nearby, unmoving. You call out to him to see if he's alive. As you wait for an answer that never comes, you slowly close your eyes for the last time.

THE END

To follow another path, turn to page 11.
To read the conclusion, turn to page 101.

63

You finish your final training with a B-25. Then your squadron ships out to a small island in the Pacific Ocean called Morotai, close to the Philippines. For your first mission, your target is the Philippine island of Mindanao, where the Japanese have an airfield. You'll fly your B-25 at low altitude and use powerful machine guns to fire at the Japanese on the ground. Then you'll drop your bombs.

As you drop down just above the treetops, Japanese anti-aircraft guns fire up at you. But their aim is bad, and they miss. Other planes in your squadron have dropped their bombs.

"They scored some direct hits," your co-pilot, Smitty, says.

"Yeah," you say, "but the smoke is so thick I can barely see the target."

You fire the B-25's machine guns as you prepare to release your bombs. With the push of a button, a ton of bombs shoot out of the plane. You pull up to begin the flight back to Morotai.

B-25s headed toward islands in the Pacific Ocean to bomb Japanese air bases.

Turn the page.

"We got 'em hard!" your radioman says, seeing that your bombs have hit the target. But your flight back might not be an easy one. Japanese Zeroes are approaching. You can't outfly them—they're faster than you. You shoot at a Zero just as he fires his cannon at you. Your B-25 takes a direct hit to the cockpit.

You feel pain in your chest and look down and see blood. "I'm hit!" you say. You feel weak. You try to warn your crew—"Get out while you ..." But you never finish the sentence. The last thing you see is the nose of your plane as it spirals into the ocean below.

66

THE END

To follow another path, turn to page 11.
To read the conclusion, turn to page 101.

"It's too risky to fly that low," you say.
You begin to turn and see two more Zeroes
approaching in the faint moonlight. You feel your
body tense. The enemy bullets hit the plane,
making a noise like hammering metal. Your
gunners fire and score several direct hits. The men
cheer as one Zero explodes. Another goes down
in a fiery streak.

"Just one left," Bill says. "And he's already taken
some hits." Still, the Zero has enough power to
fire again. An explosion tells you he's scored a hit.
"Number two engine is out," Bill says. "But that
Zero is nowhere in sight."

"How's Roy?" you radio to the back of
the plane.

"We stopped the bleeding," the bombardier
says. "He'll be OK."

Turn the page.

"Then let's get home," you say, heading back toward the base. In a few minutes, though, you feel a shudder. You've been hit again. Another engine! "Good thing we have two more," Joe says. "And I've heard some B-24s have even made it back with just one engine."

"I don't want to push our luck," you say. You feel the plane start to lose altitude. "Throw out anything we don't need," you order. You hate to lose the valuable equipment, but you have to. The lighter you are, the easier it is to fly with only two engines. The crew tosses out guns and heavy equipment. Finally, you see the lights of the air base ahead of you. You've made it back in one piece—this time.

THE END

To follow another path, turn to page 11.
To read the conclusion, turn to page 101.

68

For your new mission, you learn to fly a B-29, the newest Air Force bomber. Unlike your old B-24, the guns are fired by remote control. Also, the plane is pressurized, so you won't need to wear an oxygen mask.

After your training you and your flight group head to a huge air base on Tinian, a Pacific Island. From there your B-29 can easily reach targets in Japan. In the summer of 1945, you finally learn what the secret mission is all about.

An officer explains it to your group: "Our scientists have developed a new weapon—the atomic bomb. Just one of these bombs can destroy large parts of a city. With this bomb we can end the war—and save the lives of many American soldiers."

Turn the page.

When the final orders come, you aren't assigned to fly the *Enola Gay*, the B-29 that will carry the bomb. Instead, you're the co-pilot of another plane, the *Great Artiste*. It will carry scientists who will measure the destructive force of the bomb.

The B-29 *Enola Gay* dropped the world's first atomic bomb August 6, 1945.

On August 6 the planes take off from Tinian. Over the Japanese city of Hiroshima, the *Enola Gay* releases the atomic bomb. It drifts down on a parachute, so both planes will have time to get away before the massive explosion. In 43 seconds the explosion comes. A moment later you feel a wave of energy bounce against your plane. The bomb has worked!

You and the rest of the crew look back and see a huge cloud of thick white smoke rising tens of thousands of feet into the air. You hope the officers are right—that dropping this bomb will finally end the war.

THE END

To follow another path, turn to page 11.
To read the conclusion, turn to page 101.

Tuskegee Airman Edward Gleed
flew a P-51 Mustang in the
332nd Fighter Group.

CHAPTER 4

THE TUSKEGEE AIRMEN

It's 1943, and you have just finished high school in Boston. The United States is heavily involved in World War II, and you want to help fight. You go to a recruiting office and tell the sergeant, "I want to fly for the Army Air Force."

"What are you talking about?" the sergeant says harshly. "The Army doesn't let Negroes fly planes."

"Yes, sir, it does," you say quietly, trying not to anger the sergeant. You've grown up surrounded by whites. You know some of them are racist. "The Army began accepting Negro cadets in 1941. There's a separate airfield to train them down in Alabama."

73

Turn the page.

"Never heard of it," the sergeant says. "Look, if you want to join the Army, maybe you can be a cook."

You walk out of the office. You go to another recruiting station. Then another. None of the sergeants say they have heard of Tuskegee Institute, where black pilots are already training. Finally, you find a station where the sergeant will listen to you. He tells you to report to Fort Devens, which is near Boston. You smile.

Everything goes well at Fort Devens. Next you need to decide what kind of plane you want to fly. You like the fighters because they're fast and make you think quickly. But you also like the idea of working with a team, as you would in a bomber.

• To train as a fighter pilot, go to page 75.
• To train as a bomber pilot, turn to page 80.

74

You decide to become a fighter pilot—or at least find out if you're good enough.

Within a week you're boarding a train to go to your basic training at Keesler Air Force Base in Biloxi, Mississippi. In Washington, D.C., you change trains and take a seat. A police officer comes up to you. "You can't sit here," he says. "Come with me." The officer leads you to a dirty, noisy seat near the coal, which powers the steam engine.

Trains and public buildings are segregated in the South. Blacks and whites don't sit together, and blacks are always treated worse. You feel anger rising inside you. You want to help your country. But the country's laws treat you unfairly. You wonder when blacks will get equal rights.

Turn the page.

After your training in Mississippi, you go to Tuskegee, Alabama. Later, all the pilots who train there will be called Tuskegee Airmen. One trainer has already flown dozens of combat missions with the Airmen. "We helped sink a German warship once," he tells you. "But mostly we protect the bombers from the German fighters."

You practice in many types of planes. One of them is the T-6, which has two seats—one for the student and one for the trainer. Captain Carl Simmons asks who wants to go on a training flight. You like flying with him because you learn a lot. But you see that Leon, another cadet you know, is eager to go. He doesn't have much experience yet. Maybe you should let Leon have a chance.

• To let the other cadet fly, go to page 77.

• To go on the training flight, turn to page 93.

While escorting U.S. bombers over Europe, the Tuskegee Airmen shot down more than 100 German planes.

"You go ahead," you tell Leon. "I'll get another chance to go with the captain."

Over the next few weeks, you complete your training at Tuskegee. Your next stop is a U.S. air base in Italy. You are a member of the new 301st Fighter Squadron, part of the 332nd Fighter Group. You'll be flying one of the best fighters in the sky—the P-51 Mustang.

Turn the page.

All the planes in the group have red paint on their tails. The American bomber pilots call the Airmen "Red Tail Angels." You and the other Tuskegee pilots have won the respect of the white pilots. You're known for keeping the bombers safe.

As the months go by, you fly many missions. One day you see a different kind of German plane swooping down from the clouds above. You realize right away that it's the new plane other pilots have talked about. The Me 262 is the world's first fighter plane with a jet engine. It flies faster than anything else in the skies.

This one is closing in on you. Your Mustang can't outfly it, but you can turn more quickly.

You try to get into the best position to fire. Another Mustang flies nearby while the Me 262 turns, hoping to fire its cannons at you. Before the pilot can fire, you dive down. The bullets from his guns whistle past you.

You glance over and see an Me 109 approaching. It's not a jet plane, but it's still fast. Before you can get out of the way, its guns fire. You hear some of the bullets tear into the side of your plane.

"I'm hit," you radio to base. "Not sure how bad." Your plane is starting to lose oil. You should probably head back to base. But you don't want to go back without taking out that jet plane.

• To go after the Me 262, turn to page 87.

• To head back toward the base, turn to page 95.

In a few days, you take a train to Biloxi, Mississippi. At Keesler Air Base, you take more tests and go through basic training. Along with the flight training, you take college classes. The work is hard—much harder than high school. And the physical training is much tougher than anything you've ever done in gym. You tell James, another cadet, "I'm not sure I can make it as a pilot."

"They make it even harder for us Negroes," he says. "Some whites in the military want us to fail—just because we're black."

One day Sergeant Harvey Jones, a white airman you don't like, asks for a volunteer. "I want one of you to fly the China Clipper tomorrow morning," he says. "Who wants to do it?"

You and the other cadets look at each other. None of you have ever heard of the China Clipper. Maybe it's a new plane. It would be great to fly something new. But then you remember what another cadet once told you—never volunteer for anything in the Army. You never know what you're in for.

• To volunteer, turn to page 82.

• To keep quiet, turn to page 85.

You decide to volunteer. "Excellent," Sergeant Jones says. "I'll see you tomorrow at 0300 hours." Three o'clock in the morning! No one flies planes that early.

At 3 a.m. Jones leads you to the kitchen. He points at the dishwasher and says, "This is the China Clipper. Enjoy yourself, cadet." You see stacks of dishes all around. Maybe Jones would have tried to trick a white cadet too. But you feel that he enjoyed it more because you're black.

Now you're really not sure you want to be here at Tuskegee. The other cadets seem to know more than you, and you can't stand the racism. And maybe you're not a good enough pilot.

You find out when you go out for a check ride later that day—the flight that shows your skills. A white officer, Major Wallace Bendall, flies with you. You fly the plane through loops, rolls, and dives. But you can tell the test is not going well— the moves are not as sharp as they should be. You have a feeling you're going to wash out.

Airmen lined up for inspection at Randolph Air Force Base.

Turn the page.

The next day you get the news you were expecting. "I'm afraid you don't have what it takes to be a pilot," Major Bendall says. "But a bomber needs other crewmembers. You could be a gunner or a navigator."

You know you can still help your country on a bomber crew. But maybe you should leave the Army Air Force altogether, to escape the racism.

• To become a bomber crewmember, turn to page 90.

• To consider leaving the Army Air Force, turn to page 92.

James steps forward. You're glad you didn't volunteer, because you later learn that the China Clipper is a nickname for a dishwasher. James had to get up at 3 a.m. to wash dishes!

When your training is finished at Tuskegee, you earn your wings. You transfer to Freeman Field in Indiana. You're assigned to a squadron that is part of the 477th Bombardment Group. Now you have more training on the plane you will fly in combat—the B-25 bomber.

You've earned the rank of second lieutenant, making you an officer. In the military, officers have their own clubs where they can relax when they're not on duty. But you learn that black officers don't have equal rights. They can't use the club that white officers use.

Turn the page.

A group of black officers meets to discuss what is happening. "This is crazy," Captain Coleman Young says. "White bomber groups get sent overseas a lot faster than we do. It's like they don't want us to fight."

"Yeah," Lieutenant Harold Smith says. "And they don't face the unfair treatment we do here at home."

"We have to do something about this," Young says. "We should go into that white officers' club and demand our rights."

86

Turn to page 97.

You see the other Mustangs from your group approaching. More German planes have arrived too, and dogfights start all over the skies. You keep your eye on that first Me 262—that's the one you want. You circle around him and fire your guns. It's a direct hit! The plane tumbles to the ground.

"That's a kill," another pilot radios. "Nice shooting."

You glance down at the oil gauge. It's fallen quickly since you were hit. Just then, bullets pour into the tail of your plane. A German has come up from behind. Black smoke billows into the cockpit, choking you. Your plane is going down, and you have only one choice now—jump.

Turn the page.

To your surprise, the German fighters don't fire at you as you parachute to the ground. But as you land, you see German soldiers running toward you with guns. They take you to a prisoner of war camp called Stalag Luft III.

A German officer questions you in English. You give him the only information a prisoner is supposed to give—name, rank, and serial number.

In the camp are several thousand British and American airmen. Most of them are white. You wonder how the Americans will treat you. An American from one barracks comes over to you and shakes your hand. "I'm Airman Mike Thompson," he says in a southern drawl. "We want you to stay with us."

"OK," you say. Inside the barracks you find out why Mike wanted you.

Prisoners of war were counted during roll call twice a day at Stalag Luft III.

"The Germans sometimes sneak in one of their own men who speaks good English," he says. "They're planting spies. The Germans want to know if we're planning an escape." Mike smiles. "But I've never seen a black German pilot before, so I figured you must be one of us."

You don't know what's in store for you, but at least you're among fellow Allied airmen.

THE END

To follow another path, turn to page 11.
To read the conclusion, turn to page 101.

The major arranges for you to take some tests, to see what you could do on a bomber crew. You score well on the math skills needed to be a bombardier, so you head for training at Midland Army Air Base in Texas.

The navigator of a B-25 had a bird's-eye view from the nose of the plane.

You work with one of the first secret weapons of the war, the Norden bombsight. The device takes information you enter into it and decides the exact moment when the bombs should be released.

When your training is done, you wait for your orders to go into combat and prove your skills. But the Army is dragging its feet, just like it did with black fighter pilots, and you don't get the chance. The black bomber pilots are never sent into combat before the end of the war.

THE END

To follow another path, turn to page 11.
To read the conclusion, turn to page 101.

"You can leave the Air Force for another Army unit, if that's what you want," the major says. "But you might not like the assignment you end up with instead."

You wonder where you'll be assigned. You know that just a few Army units are integrated—blacks and whites serving together. But in many cases, the blacks get the jobs that don't take much skill. They cook food or drive trucks. But your time at Tuskegee has shown you that you're pretty smart. You'll show the Army what you can do to fight—even if it won't be from the cockpit.

92

THE END

To follow another path, turn to page 11.
To read the conclusion, turn to page 101.

"I need all the hours I can get up in the air," you say as you step forward.

"I like your attitude," Captain Simmons says with a smile. "Let's go."

You began your training in an old biplane. The T-6 you're flying today is more like the fighters used in combat. It's not as fast as a Mustang, but it can do the same kinds of moves in the air. You climb inside the cockpit behind the captain. Before you know it, you're airborne with Simmons at the controls.

"I want to show you a new move," he says. "We're going to do an inverted roll." You know what's coming—the plane will roll on its side, so for a split second you'll be flying upside down.

Turn the page.

You brace yourself for the roll. But suddenly you feel yourself falling from your seat—your seatbelt has snapped! You grab at anything you can to stay in the plane. "Captain!" you yell.

You hold on, but Captain Simmons loses control of the plane. You're filled with terror. You see the ground zooming closer through the windshield of the T-6 as it hurtles downward. You die before you ever see battle.

94

THE END

To follow another path, turn to page 11.
To read the conclusion, turn to page 101.

"I'm losing oil," you radio. "I'm turning back."
You watch the oil gauge move lower and lower.
You keep flying, looking for a field to land in—
you hope not one on German soil. You want to
reach Yugoslavia. Many people there are fighting
the Germans. The partisans help Allied pilots
when they can.

You see an open space up ahead and start to
bring the Mustang down. You go in on the plane's
belly, since it's too dangerous to land on your
wheels. You keep your speed at about 120 miles
per hour until you're just about to hit the ground.
The plane lands with a thud and bounces a few
times before sliding to a stop.

Turn the page.

A kind farmer, whose field you've landed in, helps you to his house. Because of his warm welcome you realize that he's Yugoslavian, though you can't understand what he's saying.

You don't know how long it will take you to get back to base. But at least for the moment you're alive and safe.

THE END

To follow another path, turn to page 11.
To read the conclusion, turn to page 101.

"I'll go with you into the club," you say. Young smiles and draws up a plan. On the first night several groups of officers will go into the club. The next night another group will go. You volunteer for the second group.

The first night does not go well. The black officers are arrested and forced to stay in the barracks. The next night you feel a little nervous as you and several other African-American officers enter the club. A white major is waiting for you. "You know you're not allowed in this club," he says.

You take a deep breath and find the courage to speak. "Under Army and U.S. government rules, we should be allowed in." He places you under arrest.

Turn the page.

The next day Colonel Robert Selway closes the club. Soon he writes a statement outlining the policy of separate clubs for white and black officers. He wants all the officers to sign the statement to show they accept it. You are called into a room where a white officer asks you to sign. You refuse.

Tuskegee Airmen fought racism within the military.

You soon learn that 101 black officers refused to sign Selway's policy. If you are found guilty of disobeying an order, you could go to prison and lose your rank, or worse. Soon all of you are relocated to Godman Field in Kentucky.

After a few days, on April 23, 1945, you receive good news. The top Army general, George C. Marshall, has ordered you all released. And from now on, the 477th will have a black commanding officer. But by the time this happens, the war is almost over. You will never fly a bomber in combat. But at least you know you stood up for what was right.

99

THE END

To follow another path, turn to page 11.
To read the conclusion, turn to page 101.

A British Avenger torpedo bomber flew over the HMS *Indomitable* aircraft carrier during a bombing exercise.

CHAPTER 5

BRAVERY IN THE AIR

Even before World War II began, the world's leading nations saw that planes would play a huge role in warfare. The Americans and the British focused on building bombers that could fly long distances and carry heavy loads of bombs. The Germans built planes that could help their soldiers on the battlefield.

When the United States entered the war, much of its air power was based at sea on aircraft carriers. The Japanese and U.S. navies fought the world's first sea battles in which the enemy ships could not see each other. Almost all the fighting took place between carrier-based planes.

During the war the countries tried to improve their planes when they could. The United States introduced faster fighters, such as the Hellcat and the Mustang. German pilots flew the world's first jet plane, called the Swallow (Me 262).

A new U.S. bomber, the B-29, dropped bombs that caused deadly fires in Japanese cities. B-29s also dropped the world's first atomic bombs, killing or wounding several hundred thousand people. Those bombs helped end the war with Japan.

RAF flyers returned home after a successful mission.

103

Just as important as the planes used were the pilots who flew them. They carried out many kinds of missions while facing enemy fire from land and from other planes. They learned how to fire their guns, drop bombs and torpedoes, and avoid enemy planes. They parachuted out if their planes got hit. And at times pilots and their crews crash-landed. At sea, they risked drowning. They also faced capture by the enemy and becoming prisoners of war.

The pilots of World War II showed great bravery and skill as they carried out their missions. And the pilots known as the Tuskegee Airmen battled racism in their struggle to help defend their country. The U.S. military ended segregation in 1948, so anyone with the skills can now be a pilot.

Today's military pilots fly faster planes with better technology. But like the pilots of World War II, they rely on courage and talent to survive the dangers of war.

TIMELINE

1903—The first airplane flight takes place.

1914—World War I starts.

1918—World War I ends, and Germany is soon forced to give up most of its military.

1933—Adolf Hitler comes to power in Germany and begins secretly building a new air force.

1939—On September 1 German troops invade Poland, starting World War II.

1940—Germany takes control of France in June after invading other western European nations.

In August German planes begin a major attack on Great Britain, known as the Battle of Britain.

1941—On December 7 Japanese planes attack Pearl Harbor, Hawaii, bringing the United States into World War II.

1942—The first Tuskegee Airmen receive their wings and become military pilots.

The Battle of the Coral Sea marks the first time enemy naval ships battle each other without seeing each other; planes based on aircraft carriers do the fighting.

1944—German pilots fly the world's first jet-powered airplane.

In July Tuskegee Airmen fly P-51 Mustang fighters for the first time.

On March 11 a kamikaze damages the USS *Randolph*, killing 25 crewmen.

1945—In April members of the 477th Bombardment Group, made up of Tuskegee Airmen, protest segregation at Freeman Field, Indiana.

World War II ends in Europe on May 8, V-E (Victory in Europe) Day.

On August 6 a B-29 bomber called the *Enola Gay* drops the world's first atomic bomb on Hiroshima; another atomic bomb is dropped on Nagasaki three days later.

World War II ends in Asia on August 14.

1948—President Harry Truman ends segregation in the military.

OTHER PATHS TO EXPLORE

In this book you've seen how the events of the past look different from three points of view. Perspectives on history are as varied as the people who lived it. Seeing history from many points of view is an important part of understanding it.

Here are ideas for other World War II points of view to explore:

+ You are a female pilot flying planes for the RAF or the U.S. Army Air Force. You take planes where they are needed and help pilots and anti-aircraft gunners train. In Great Britain you take the planes to the front lines. How would you feel if male pilots said women shouldn't be allowed to fly?

+ You are a German bomber pilot setting off for England during the Blitz. You know your target is a city filled with civilians—including many women and children. How do you feel about having to attack them?

+ More than 40,000 members of the Army Air Force were captured by the enemy during World War II, usually after being shot down. These prisoners of war often suffered harsh treatment. What would it have been like to be a POW held by the Germans or Japanese?

READ MORE

Gitlin, Martin. *World War II on the Home Front: An Interactive History Adventure.* Mankato, Minn: Capstone Press, 2012.

Grant, Reg. *World War II: The Events and Their Impact on Real People.* New York: DK Pub., 2008.

Senker, Cath. *Why Did World War II Happen?* New York: Gareth Stevens Publishing, 2011.

Williams, Brian. *Pilots in Peril.* Chicago: Heinemann Library, 2012.

INTERNET SITES

Use FactHound to find Internet sites related to this book. All of the sites on FactHound have been researched by our staff.

Here's all you do:

Visit *www.facthound.com*

Type in this code: 9781429698993

GLOSSARY

atomic bomb (uh-TAH-mik BOM)—a weapon that uses nuclear power to create massive destruction

barracks (BEAR-uhks)—housing for soldiers

bombardier (bahm-buh-DEER)—a bombing crew member who controls where and when bombs drop from airplanes

cadet (kuh-DET)—a military student

deferment (di-FER-ment)—approved postponement of required military service

racist (RAY-sist)—prejudice or discrimination against a person or group of a different race

rudder (RUHD-ur)—a metal plate attached to a plane to help the pilot steer

segregated (SEG-ruh-gay-ted)—separated by race

squadron (SKWAHD-ruhn)—a unit of the military

throttle (THROT-uhl)—a lever, pedal, or handle used to control the speed of an engine

wash out (WASH OUT)—fail to pass the training program to become a pilot

wingman (WING-man)—pilot who flies behind and to the side of the leader of a group of planes

BIBLIOGRAPHY

Arthur, Max. *Last of the Few: The Battle of Britain in the Words of the Pilots Who Won It*. New York: Skyhorse Publishing, 2011.

Battle of Britain 1940. BBC. 2 Oct. 2012. www.bbc.co.uk/ww2peopleswar/categories/c55221/.

Battle of Britain 70th Anniversary. Royal Air Force. 2 Oct. 2012. www.raf.mod.uk/history/battleofbritain70thanniversary.cfm.

Bush, George. *All the Best, George Bush: My Life in Letters and Other Writings*. New York: Scribner, 1999.

Griggs, Alan L., ed. *Flying Flak Alley: Personal Accounts of World War II Bomber Crew Combat*. Jefferson, N.C.: McFarland, 2008.

Holland, James. *The Battle of Britain: Five Months That Changed History, May–October 1940*. New York: St. Martin's Press, 2011.

Moye, J. Todd. *Freedom Flyers: The Tuskegee Airmen of World War II*. New York: Oxford University Press, 2010.

Royal Air Force. BBC. 2 Oct. 2012. www.bbc.co.uk/ww2peopleswar/categories/c1183/index.shtml.

Sears, David. *Pacific Air: How Fearless Flyboys, Peerless Aircraft, and Fast Flattops Conquered a Vast Ocean's Wartime Skies*. Cambridge, Mass.: Da Capo Press, 2011.

INDEX